Adopt a Yak

by Alex Yu
illustrated by Mick Reid

Practice Decodable 49

I0806519

McGraw Hill Education

Bothell, WA • Chicago, IL • Columbus, OH • New York, NY

MHEonline.com

Copyright © 2015 McGraw-Hill Education

All rights reserved. No part of this publication may be reproduced or distributed in any form or by any means, or stored in a database or retrieval system, without the prior written consent of McGraw-Hill Education, including, but not limited to, network storage or transmission, or broadcast for distance learning.

Send all inquiries to:
McGraw-Hill Education
8787 Orion Place
Columbus, OH 43240

ISBN: 978-0-02-138917-9
MHID: 0-02-138917-9

Printed in China.

8 9 10 11 12 DSS 27 26 25 24 23

Pals went to Canyon Animal Park.
"Let's adopt a yak!" yelled Yasmin.

"Can kids adopt an animal?" asked Tim.

"Yes," Yasmin said.

"It costs a lot," said Liz.

"Let's sell things," said Yasmin.

The kids sold things for cash.
Stuff filled Yasmin's yard!

The yard had lots of things.
"Help us adopt a yak!" yelled Tim.

Did the pals get the cash?

Yes, they did!